ㄣ

THIS
IS
WHERE

D1603800

poems

LOUISE K. WAAKAA'IGAN

Willow Books, a Division of Aquarius Press

Detroit, Michigan

This is Where: Poems

Copyright © 2020 by Louise K. Waakaa'igan

Editor: Randall Horton

Cover art: "Dragon Fly Moon" by Dyani White Hawk

ISBN 978-1-7330898-1-4

Willow Books, a Division of Aquarius Press

www.WillowLit.net

Printed in the United States of America

for Marie Angeline and Alexander Sage,

because

This is Where

Preface

I have been writing *This Is Where* for what seems an excruciating amount of time. It has only been, in part, through my incarceration that I have been able to sit with the experiences of my life and put them to words, not just for my writing, but for my understanding and healing. I do not believe I am at the end of this road of discovery. Yet, I have begun.

What a journey it has been. Mi'iw.

Introduction

In this eagerly anticipated volume Anishinaabekwe poet Louise K. Waakaa'igan lets us hear the "winds of flutes" even as she writes from "concrete plains" of prison. In the tradition of political prisoners Leonard Peltier and Marilyn Buck, this poet lets word fly through and beyond prison walls. A multilayered origin story, *This is Where* refuses to duck the contradictions of time, place, belonging. She writes, "I'm from women with the same last name / and a father/ none of us knew." His early abandonment leaves his daughter jostling questions:

> I'm left handed   Was he?
> My hair curls.   His?
> I give up.   Why did he?

With these yearnings, Waakaa'igan does the inner work of a poet, first, as she bravely admits "I walk out on others dad, / desperately / mimicking /you." But then the poet refuses that lonely journey, her poems, a reclaiming of her family, home, self. Through the volume we see her move from "I am a woman gray / within shadows/ losing my sense of normalcy" to "home / where I long to be. / Miles away under the same brave moon / my home   the shelter/ I abandoned too soon." We watch her mourn lost time with her grandmother, mother and son—"I still smell your morning breath." And we see her track down origins of shame in "Things I Will Carry, "scars from the basement of the yellow house,/ my first home."

In "I'm Okay," the poet writes, "My body quivers to the absence of power" (how beautiful is that line), and "sadness/ of your exodus/ scars my entire body." And yet, through the grit of wanting, her insistence on health, Waakaa'igan also writes, "you/ I lay down/my sorrows/ you/ I forgive." She asks what we all ask with the distilled grace of a poet, "Will I be what I crave?"   And then three lines down that one word proclamation: *Free*. She specifies "I am not home / on the flight pattern of *migizi* wings / I am the eagle."

This is Where invites its audience into Waakaa'igan's inner life, intertwined with world struggles, violence against Indigenous people, the degradation of the earth. She writes, "angels vacated / this atmosphere moons back, / before climate change / needed an Ojibwe translation." Standing with Madonna Thunder Hawk, Winona La Duke and other Native women activists, Waakaa'igan names "historical trauma,/ demolishing oil pipes / piercing my tribal homeland." As a woman enrolled at Odaawaa Zaaga 'iganing (Lac Courte Orielles Reservation) in North Wisconsin she stands with the land, river, sea- and mountain protectors of the world.

Like Turkish political prisoner poet Nakim Hikmet in his poem "Some Advice for Those of Us Who Will Serve Time in Prison" (1949) Waakaa'igan knows that time spent inside must wrap around beauty in order to survive. Hikmet writes, "It's not that you can't pass / ten twenty years inside / and more--, you can/ as long as the jewel at the left side of your chest does not lose its luster!" *This is Where* offers us words that luster, reminding all sentient beings to stay present, not get overwhelmed. In "Her, Gauwiin" she writes, "When/the ghost of tomorrow/begs me/to lay with you,/ I bolt/ my eyes shut." This challenge, to nourish presence even as gray walls invade the senses, gives a 21st century example of Chrystos' *Not Vanishing* and Beth Brant's *A Gathering of Spirit*, the first anthology of poetry by and for North American Indian Women (1984). In the introduction to that volume Quinte Mohawk editor Beth Brant writes, "Because in the unraveling, the threads become more, apparent, each one with its distinct color and texture. And as I unravel, I also weave."

With *This Is Where*, the reader knows we are in the presence of a precious word weaver. It's no wonder—and so much hard work—that Waakaa'igan is the recipient of the 2017 PEN America Prison Writing Awards Poetry Prize for her first place poem, "This is Where," (featured in this volume) and the 2018 Willow Books Chapbook Award. With playful and wise line breaks Waakaa'igan writes in the Joy Harjo's *A Map to the Next World*, conjuring joy through imagination, sound. As she weaves Ojibwe and English into her heart-searing poems Waaka'gan gives us an alphabet that wiggles its way toward feedom. *This is Where* offers inspired, sad, lonesome, original, surprising poems, a chapbook from a woman who makes a promise to her spine "I will keep /us free." —*Becky Thompson*

Within

I am woman gray
  within shadows
    losing my sense of normalcy
through the monotony that freezes my
    already cold spine —
      my hands never warm.
Am I not created for more?

The crude cement cell block erases the moon.
  my dreams sense no guidance
    my tears no destination
      my scars —   still wound.
When will my ancestral guide return?

I carve my sternum, carve
    the holiness out, ceasing my breath,
      the genesis of my fear.
I am not home.

Where is my *bimaadiziwin*?

I am a foreigner
in my own land, a ghostless shadow begging
  to be remembered for more
than solitude.

Where are my well-worn moccasins
  To guide me home?

11

Who will carry this desolation
When these *migizi* wings are too dirty
from thundering storms?

Savior—
        I am within
my kaleidoscope breaking and failing
        my heartbeat.
                        Again.

Ni mama—
        I miss your home.
Ningozis—
        I still smell your morning breath.
Abba—
                I.

nothing to remember,
all she has of
her father is
herself

Transition
to poem
about
father

12

Mine

What I know of my father:
    He was in the Navy.
    He worked at our tribe's casino. Security.
    He had cancer.
    He left me.
    Twice.

What I do not know of my father:
    If he held me.
    What he remembered.
    Were there regrets?
    Why he left?
    Everything.

Almost stranger, this man
whose name I carry
    held my son. My child,
whose veins flow with my blood,
    my father's blood.

My father, with his slouched frame
    held my son's tiny, perfect toes.
        I watched.
My father.
    My son.

This is void of sound.
I do not remember his voice. I do not remember his words
    only
this one soundless memory.

Are words necessary?

Pieces

The bones of my father
no longer heal.

   The bones of
my skeleton brave
      their own vision quests.

I have no war stories,
no drunken survival methods.
Only an empty canvas,
      repeating dreams
   of his disappearance.

This is what I see.
This is what I know.
He is what
      I remember.
He is what I do
   not remember.

Things I Will Carry

Scripture cards from both New Testament
and Old. They help me
    remember.
Scars from the basement of the yellow house,
    my first home.
Sweet grass bundles,
photos of *ningozis*– young.
  Ernie's shadows.
Historical trauma,
dental floss,
wretched vows of integrity.
Birthday candles,
Louise's memory,
ni mama's sorrow,
  and her blessing.
Paper,
pens,
asemaa.

The Day I Choose Nokomis' Name

Too much emotional care
    is foreign in my family.
Yet, my mother said it,

    My mom would be so proud.

With a smile on my mother's patient face,
    her hands held an Ojibwe dictionary —
        she was ready.
Ready to show the Judge written
    proof of our oral language, waakaa'igan.

    My mom would be so proud.

Except,
    my shackles,
the metal restraints steeling my fragile
    body
to the Department of Corrections
    and the State of Minnesota
Yet, my mother said it,

    My mom would be so proud.

This Is Where

I'm from *Bineshi's* bloodline.
That's – Bill Baker – if you don't speak Ojibwemowin.
     Ni migizi dodem.

I'm from Six Mile.
49n up the driveway, sitting on green
     boxes watching cars.
Sometimes their doors didn't match.

I'm from Packer games on Sundays,
Greyhound trips for Christmas,
and Easter baskets with Karla.

I'm from women with the same last name
     and a father
          none of us knew.

I'm from the woods: northern.
Where pines and birch bark blanket
both bends of tribal roads,
     paved and gravel.

I'm from a single-parent household.
Michael Jackson cassette tapes,
   Purple Rain posters and latch–key kids.
Title V programs, commods on pantry shelves,
     cucumbers from Grandpa Jake's garden
and a mean ol' dog name Turkey.

pride, perhaps

I'm from "crying won't change anything" and

17

"you should've known better."

I'm from punitive silence
    and where it's normal.
Hugs are warm and forced Catholicism still
weighs heavy on *ni mama's* shoulders.

Commonality Between Tribes

I watched tears drop
down her cheeks as she shielded her tattooed, skinny arms
    over her slouched frame.
I kept my head down,
    aware of others
around us.
    She fought those tears,
blatant, submissive combat.

We were not in a prison dayroom
anymore; she took me beyond
    to the gravesite of her deceased.
    I didn't ask to go.
I wanted distance between us.

She spoke of death,
and its aftermath
on her life
    and posture.
Sitting by her side, I wasn't
thinking of her pain.
I went to the yellow house in six mile,
    the last house I seen Bobby alive in.

I didn't get distance from her. She
didn't make peace with her tears.

Silence betrayed us both.

Rendering

There are no angels on this
porcelain figurine shelf.
    Only hardened clay far removed
from her earthen home.
    Rudimentary remains
of divine roots dislocate
      when you hold her
      just right

under a setting sun,
late in *dagwaagin*.

    Gauwiin,

angels vacated
this atmosphere moons backs,
      before climate change
needed an Ojibwe translation.

Father

I could make up a story,
    draw you in
with powerful imagery.
Then,
        I leave you.

I am attracted to beginnings.

Eighteen
    years later,
I walked out on him.
        He was
drunk   I wasn't.

I walked away
        after
looking at his shoes.

What shoes
    would make a father walk
for eighteen years away
from his youngest
    daughter?

I hated those shoes.
    I hated his hands.
His slouched shoulders.
        The pity drenched
    in his liquored slur.
The generic cigarettes he smoked.

I hated him.   *call and response*

I'm left handed.   Was he?

My hair curls.   His?

I give up.   Why did he?

Then

    I knew.

I was the daughter of a man

I did not know, but hated.

I walked away.

    His initial lesson.

mania

I'm Okay.

haunting
isolating
not being able to
explain experiences ✗

I call my friend today —

This silence voice is s c r e a m i n g.
My body in tantrums
        it hasn't seen since I was three,
eyes burdened
my mind collapsed in this confinement

        There   is   no   exit.
How are you… she asks again.

    ravaging in confusion
    weeping with lost souls
    silencing secrets
    laughing mindless memories
    in these cell-infested days,   **I**
    I lied in prison today.

I'm becoming a vegetarian… she says.
    I do not smile.
    My body quivers to the absence of powder
                coping with the addition of another powder.
    My bones protrude my skin as death tantalizes the lonely.
    I've blurred my vision.   **I**
    I cried in prison today.

I revel with Billie Holiday
        pheenin' for one more hit.
Plastic razors feed demons
        who crave,   one   more —

23

I deny myself. Because really...
    who gives a shit.
I died in prison today.

I don't discuss my time,
    my friends can't handle it.
I won't discuss this crime,
    my ego won't bury it.
I wear a pretty smile,
    Department of Corrections rehabilitates it.
I remain discipline-free,
    my family condones it.

 I prefer to be alone,
    my loved ones misunderstand it.
  I want to go Home to my brother,
    my Creator hasn't cured it.   I

    I'll survive in prison today.

How are you?   She asks —
Oh. I'm okay.

Iri

For the one I'll never hold.

you   I lay down

my sorrows.   you

    I forgive

the patterns of wind

    drawing me

nearer muddy waters

dissolving in your

shadow lines.   I

deserted me

    moons back —

Am I losing her again?

you keep

    seduction at bay.   I search

    for your   senses   for you.

Take me

into yourself.

Trace

    the beginning

of my ribs

    if only...

No, I Am Not

after Leonard Peltier

If my guilt makes me holy,
why must I feel dirty,
    — shame ridden,
        — empty,

            — so *Indian?*
Where is this redemption that I seek?
      Redemption my grandparents' grandparents died for?

I only see
      commod cans, reservation
    pride, hand-me-downs,
  and borrowed moccasins.

Will I be what I crave?

           Free.

These reservation borders intersect
family lines blending
   Amnishinaabe and (denied) European
     blood.

I am not at home
   on the flight pattern of *migizi* wings
     I am the eagle.

I wasn't born with those dreams, *gauwiin*.
Sweet grass burned
 them into my wretched soul
   the winter of 1979.
My first winter.

No, I am not holy.

Her, Gauwiin

When
the ghost of tomorrow
   begs me
to lay with you,
    I bolt
  my eyes shut —
failing to pacify her.

  I am used to this cold. My hands never warm.
I know how to walk alone.

I share secrets with the moon,
    then curse
the wind reminding me
how alone I am.
Still.

I will forget
certain things about you,
    the surprise of your first kiss,
the elementary proposal in the library.
That which I cherish the most
  the letters,
    your hands,
    your nickname,   those
will leave first —
    It will be my healing request.

The outlines of our bodies vanished
from the ink
    well, and I am
breathing again.

Facility Bred

I've become
         an empty shell case in an abandoned room.
  Rigidly lonesome
far from lonely highways
I have travelled before. I recognize
       this pattern.
This seduction —
   I am my own herion.
Laying bare
      — stolen.

  I burn with anger.
I yearn to fight
    to bleed, create new brave scars
standing in snow tracks in these concrete plains —

I am desert sand, proud with no water.
A pipe carrier
    with no elder — David has passed.
    I am without.
Those thundering storms
      won. Alone
  I stand
resting in steel chains,
    losing the woman I wanted to be.

Break Me

why today
in this gray atmosphere
          do I hear
winds of flutes
          reminding my pulse
to continue
beating?   why
must I
          listen?

this fractured mind dissolves
          in salty dimensions
of institutionalized fear
          manipulating
memories of my fatherless journeys —

may I
          plant lilies and cherry blossoms,
entwining thyme
and sage as *ni mama* did?

Remember

Once
on a cold cement staircase,
under a welcoming sunrise,
        he bit me.
Repeatedly, emptying
    boozy sorrow on my pale flesh,
destroying me.
Freeing relentless scavengers
scarring me deep
        within.
        Is this my destiny?

        *

Occasionally
I marvel at the corruptive, shy
bruises invading my privacy.
    I will survive.

        *

    I am a contradiction. Broken
and healing,
        miraculously,
                pitifully.

My Name

My name holds years
        of contorted friendships bound
by the English alphabet.
A twist —
       yesterday's normalcy,
tomorrow's uniqueness.

My name is common where
        common is true
to who sing their own
        destiny.
A holy remembrance
      of a leader
whose voice I
      yearn to hear.

Nokomis cradles my
    name she echoed
to her daughter
          her daughter.
My name,
    the lullaby cherished
by my grandchildren,

the whisper on
      my husband's lips.

Nine Years Ago
I.

Nine years ago

                                 I was twenty-three.

Nine years ago

                                 I watched a man get shot.

Nine years ago
       I pled guilty to a crime   nine years ago,

        I didn't believe   I was guilty of.

Nine years ago
                I was all I was concerned about.

Nine years ago,
                I couldn't see seven years
       into the future.   Because
    nine years ago,
    one of my criminal charges   demanded forty years.

I couldn't
      even see forward seven.

No connection
    between my mind and heart.
No awareness of
    thoughts to words,
words to actions,
actions character.

Nine years ago,
        I was a victim of myself
    and everyone to blame.

II.

Yes,   I am moving
on beyond
          my crime,
beyond
          that   one   night.

          I am moving on.

Complex and unforgiving — in part.
          It is my choosing.
In part,
  my mother's instruction.

Nine years ago
          she told me,
     "Life goes on."
I was shattered
          by that cold,
unforgiveable statement.
Nine years ago.

Today, praise God
     for that statement.
Today, praise God
     for my mother.
It means,
          life goes on.
It means
          it is no longer
nine years ago.

You

Though I
honor our
curls, I refuse to comb them.

I hate this insecurity
you've left within me.
I made peace
with the manic
depression. Yet

I stumble
on a broken foundation,
staying
close to my siblings
and their children. I disassociate

with your name, our name.
But my son carries
House well. I

blame you.
All my suspicions
infidelities,
betrayals,
abandonment,
you proved faithful.

The sadness
of your exodus

scars my entire body.

I walk out on others   dad,
desperately
    mimicking   *feeling like she's
you.   →   let people down*

booby love

My Spine

I long to bathe you
  expel the harshness
of this imprisoned
reality
  from the strength
of your structure.

I thank you,
  even in my pitiful slouch…
  I thank you.
Intentional stretches,
calming breaths,
 washing of the water…

I choose you, listen
  to you, open to you.
— lengthening hope.
  Strengthen me
as I
  solidify me
as I
  guide my purpose.

I will keep
 us free.

Inside

There is no movement.
    Each maple and golden locust limb weighs
heavy with Christian
      snow.
Concealing the bark and its impurities,
    redemption expels
layers of manmade sin.
    Legends of grace —
      Holy grace, sustaining anemic *Anishinaabe*
    bodies inside stone penitentiaries.

As each night beckons, so too my demons,
seduction
    in unwanted lands
throughout still rivers of frozen purity —

This is my *biboon*.

Weweni

What a wake of a thunderstorm —
fractured pine branches,
disintegrated leaves
    rotten,
returning to
    the dampened earth —
tangled within dissolves
    of silenced Six Mile secrets

etching steps throughout
    graveyards and reservation allotments
of historical trauma,
      — demolishing oil pipes
piercing my tribal homeland.

Uninvited

Craving
      the rhythm of you.
   Haunted
       by your touch that has not left
   its wake on my pale skin.
Breaking
     under my shadow
burning the mystery created between
you and I.

This breath would have traveled
to know you
   would call my body
      home.

  These shoulders would have held
you while we abandon
    fear from our foreign spines.

We could have made the stars
breathe as we returned
   our bodies back
to the moon.

Still

I long to remember who
    I was before the shattering
of my identity and
my hymen —

Soul – wounded,
    I search for more
than my existence as a fatherless child.

        Was I attracted to despondency then
            as I am now?   *yes.*
        Was I yearning for the darkness
            of seclusion and tar swept rooftops?   *yes.*

I am still searching for my father.

Six Mile

Home is
County Road CC,
   socks missing, keys hiding, tea cups breaking,
the doorknob falling off, again.
      — a cluttered mess with plush carpeting.

Home
   sitting on the green boxes.
The DeMarr's, the Corbine's, Lind's house,
   the brown house — I never did go inside.

Home
     turning the heat down while we sleep
and in the morning, turning it up again.   *cold in prison,*

                              privilege to turn on
Home   *heat*

where I long to be.
     Miles away, under the same brave moon —
my home   the shelter
     I abandoned too soon.

Acknowledgments

Nitam, I must give a Chi-miigwech to the following journals and publications where the poems listed below originally appeared and in earlier form:

> *Doors Adjacent*, "For November"; *27th Letter*, "Mine," "Remember," "No, I am Not"

> "Within" was the first place winner of the Minnesota Prison Writing Workshop (MPWW) Broadside competition in 2016

> *21 Anthologies*, "This Is Where"

I humbly acknowledge Randall Horton and Willow Books for publishing this collection.

Many thanks I extend to both Becky Thompson and Dyani White Hawk for supporting this project with their own creative work and brave expressions of truth.

I gratefully acknowledge Jennifer Bowen-Hicks and the mentors and teachers from within the Minnesota Prison Writing Workshop, in no particular order: Rachel M., Michael T., Heidi C., and my personal mentor Paige.

My deepest regards to the Loft Literary Center and to the late Cheri Register. She was an inspiring writer and teacher and shared her knowledge and courageous spirit with myself and others who met in the name of writing. May her spirit continue to rest in peace and her words live long.

I must include the founding women of the Writer's Workshop who selflessly encouraged and cultivated my earlier days as a writer: Malia Burkhart and Mankwe Ndosi.

To all the writers, mentors, encouragers, friends who sat in writing circle after writing circle with me and this collective love of craft. To you, to all of you, I humbly thank you. If anyone can or will consider me a writer, it is because I have had writers right alongside me, walking with me. This has never been a solo project.

In closing, I must honor the humble strength of *ni mama*, who even in my darkest of days, bestowed her beautiful light onto my life. This is because of her.

And finally, to the brightest star I have ever held, ningozis, Alexander Sage. It is all because of your empathetic heart that I have reason to excel forward. You are the beat within my heart.

Ojibwe Translations

Anishinaabe	*the Original People*
Asema	*tobacco*
Biboon	*winter*
Bimaadiziwin	*good way of life*
Daagwaagin	*autumn*
Gauwiin	*no*
Migizi	*eagle*
Nakomis	*my grandmother*
Ningozi	*my son*
Ni mama	*my mother*
Ni migizi dodem.	*I am the eagle clan.*
Miigwech	*thank you*
Ojibwemowin	*Ojibwe language*
Waakaa'igan	*house*

The dictionary I used for the translations of the Ojibwe words was *A Concise Dictionary of Minnesota Ojibwe*, edited by John Nichols and Eryl Nyholm, University of Minnesota Press, 1995. Any mistake with spelling is mine alone. As a student myself of this complex and beautiful language, I am indebted to the many who continue to speak, teach, and make accessible Ojibwemowin, not only, for us all today, but for our children in the years to come. Miigwech.

About the Poet

Louise K. Waakaa'igan (Karol House) is enrolled at Odaawaa Zaaga 'iganiing (Lac Courte Orielles) Reservstion in northern Wisconsin. Louise is the recipient of the 2017 PEN Poetry first place prize for her poem, "This Is Where." She is the first place winner of the Minnesota Prison Writing Workshop (MPWW) Broadside competition in 2016 with her poem, "Within." Louise's work has been published in PEN America's *21 Mythologies; The Moon Magazine; Doors Adjacent; 27th letter; Words in Gray Scale;* and *The Asian American Writers' Workshop: A World Without Cages.* This is her first collection.

How can I connect Ear Hustle to abroader context?

At its most basic sense, Ear Hustle makes these guys look like ordinary people - they are just ordinary people.

   - using "it's just like outside"